FULL-COLOR HISTORIC TEXTILE DESIGNS

M. Dupont-Auberville

DOVER PUBLICATIONS, INC.

NEW YORK

Bibliographical Note

This Dover edition, first published in 1995, is a republication of the plates from *l'Ornement des Tissus: Recueil Historique et Pratique,* as described in the Publisher's Note, which has been written specially for the Dover edition.

DOVER *Pictorial Archive* SERIES

Library of Congress Cataloging-in-Publication Data

Dupont-Auberville, A.
   [Ornement des tissus. English]
   Full color historic textile designs / m. Dupont-Auberville.
      p.   cm. — (Dover pictorial archive series)
   "Republication of the plates from l'Ornement des tissus: recueil historique et pratique"—T.p. verso.
   ISBN 0-486-28718-1 (pbk.)
   1. Textile design.   I. Title.
NK8804.D913   1995
677—dc20   95-10905
                                                     CIP

Manufactured in the United States of America
Dover Publications, Inc., 31 East 2nd Street, Mineola, N.Y. 11501

PUBLISHER'S NOTE

The process of lithography, invented at the end of the eighteenth century, created a new medium that was developed by such artists as Delacroix, Daumier, Manet, Degas, Toulouse-Lautrec and Redon, and also served more practical purposes, such as technical illustration. Chromolithography, a mechanical means of color reproduction, was invented in the 1830s, and by the 1860s it played a major role in printing, becoming so elaborate that a single plate might entail the use of up to 30 lithographic stones. The process was particularly useful for the design books that were published in abundance during the last three decades of the century. Mass production had created an insatiable market for all sorts of products, from housewares to textiles—all of which needed decoration. Designers required sourcebooks as references to maintain their inspiration.

Reproduced on the following pages are the plates of one such work, originally published by Ducher et Cie, Paris, in 1877 under the title *l'Ornement des Tissus: Recueil Historique et Pratique* (The ornamentation of textiles; a historical and practical collection). The plates were drawn by Charles Kreutzberger and lithographed by an individual identified only as Régamey (probably either Frédéric or Louis-Pierre-Guillaume) and were printed by the Librairie Ancienne & Moderne, Bachelin-Deflorenne. The general introduction and notes on the plates are omitted from the present edition. The captions are translations based on the originals.

FULL-COLOR HISTORIC
TEXTILE DESIGNS

1. Egyptian linen and wool.

2. First century A.D. Examples of textiles taken from wall paintings, Pompeii.

3. First through eighth centuries. Lozenges, circles and bands. From catacombs and early churches.

4. First through seventh centuries. "Consular" silks with circular motifs depicting arena games and military triumphs.

5. Eighth to eleventh centuries. Carolingian silks.

6. Eleventh century and following. Silks in circular patterns.

7. Thirteenth century. Decorated horizontal bands.

8. Thirteenth century. Birds affronté and passant.

9. Thirteenth century. Lions.

10. Thirteenth century. Silks with angels.

11. Thirteenth and fourteenth centuries. Sacred Persian tree flanked by cheetahs and other animals.

12. Fourteenth century. Silks with birds, animals and foliage.

13. Fourteenth century. German silks with animals affronté and passant.

14. Fourteenth through fifteenth centuries. Silks with vine branches.

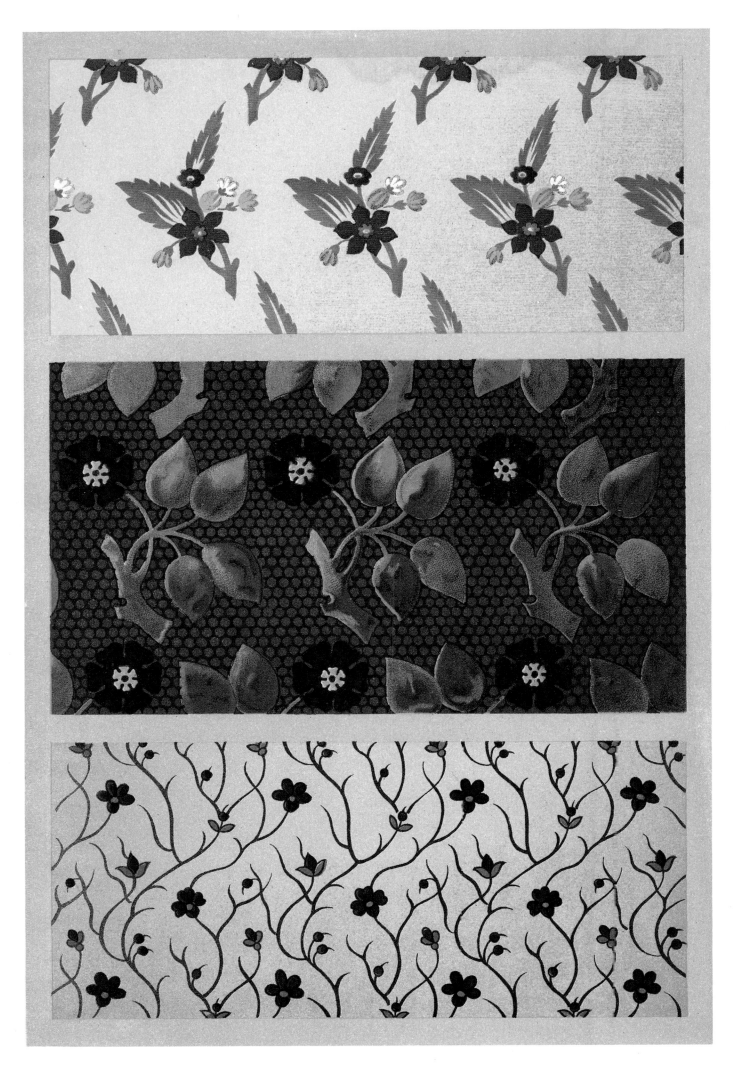

15. Fourteenth century. Branches of flowering asters.

16. Fourteenth century. Asters.

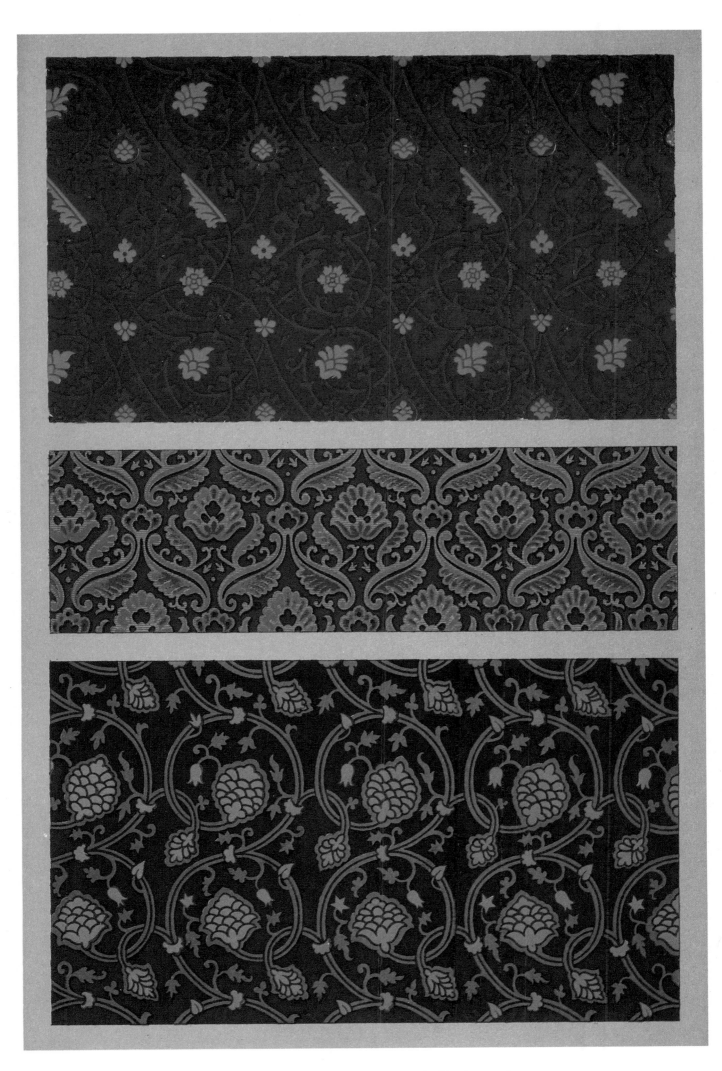

17. Fourteenth century. Patterns inspired by ironwork.

18. Fourteenth and fifteenth centuries. Polychrome velvets.

19. Fifteenth century. Italian imitations of Oriental fabrics.

20. Fifteenth century. Gothic waved panels.

21. Fifteenth century. Gothic lobed foliage.

22. End of the fifteenth through the sixteenth centuries. Gothic lobed foliage on stalks.

23. Sixteenth century. Velvets with pomegranates.

26. Sixteenth century. Silks with double strapwork borders.

27. Sixteenth century. Patterns with ribbons and crowns.

28. Sixteenth century. Renaissance silks in reticulated patterns.

29. Sixteenth century. Spanish and Italian brocatelles in panels of curving foliage.

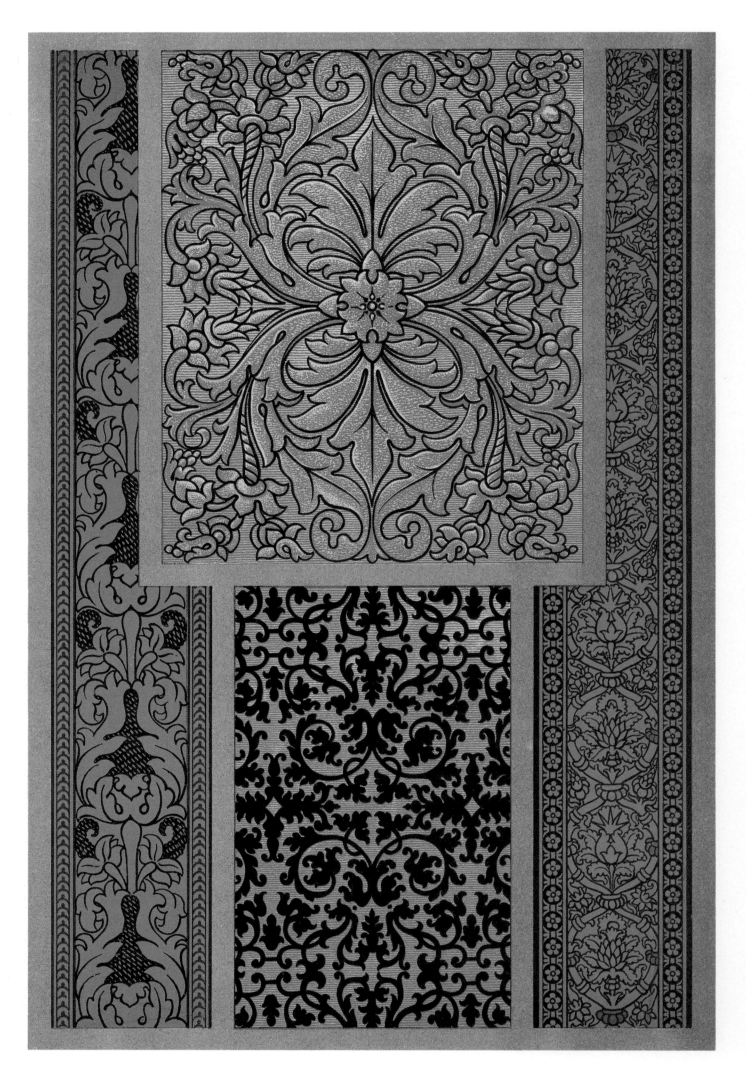

30. Sixteenth century. Looped velvet.

31. Sixteenth century. Spanish and Italian brocatelles with panels of varicus scrollings.

32. Sixteenth century. Ornamental divisions.

33. Sixteenth century. Silks and velvets in geometrical divisions.

34. Sixteenth century. Silks, velvets and damasks in small divisions.

35. Sixteenth century. Spanish silks in circular designs.

36. Sixteenth century. Velvets with fleurons.

37. Sixteenth century. Velvets with tied branches.

38. Sixteenth century. Small designs with fleurons.

39. Sixteenth century. Velvets with palms with opposed points.

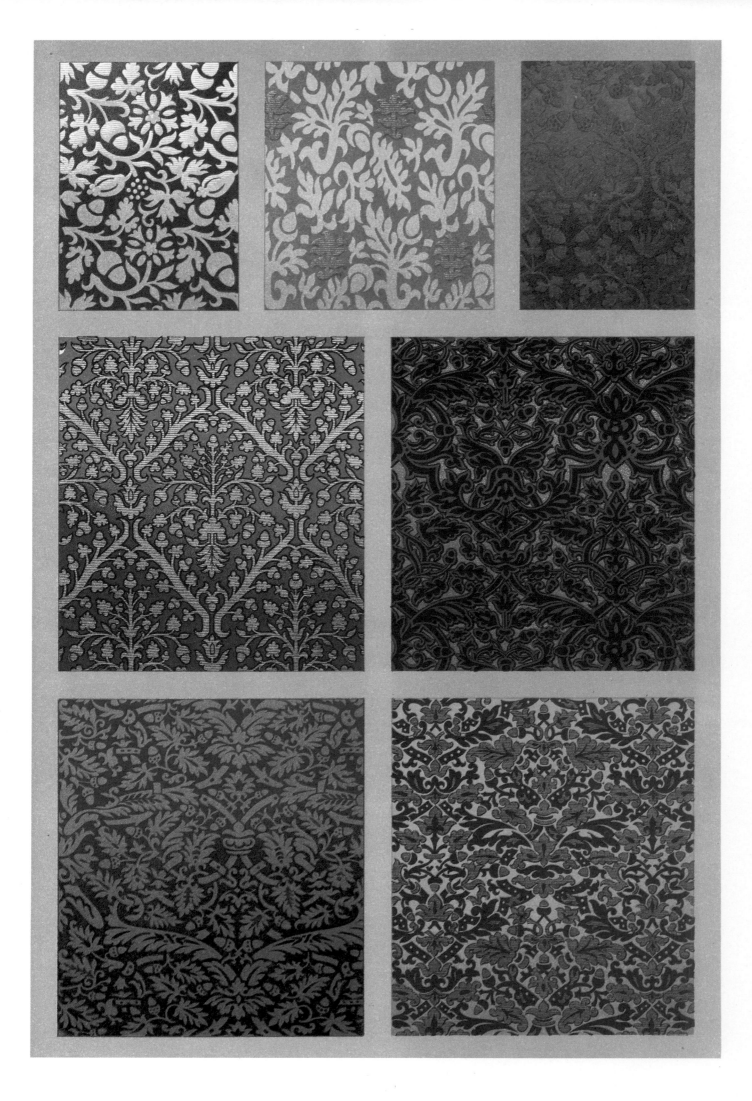

40. Sixteenth century. Oak branches.

41. Sixteenth century. Velvets with truncated branches.

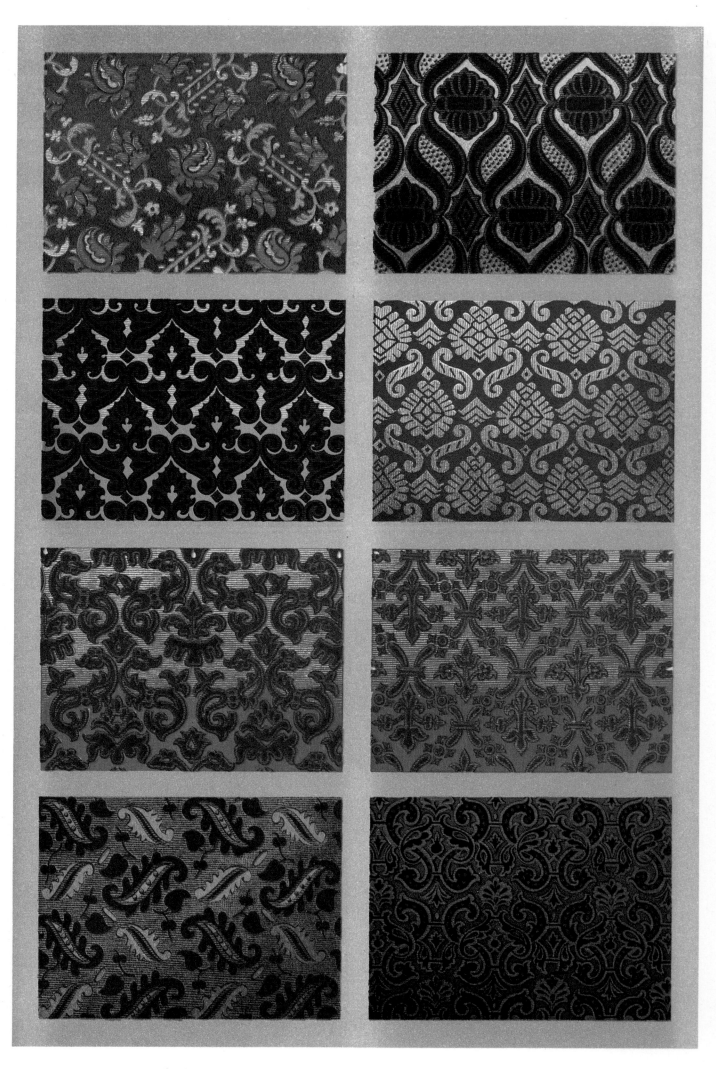

42. Sixteenth century. Silks, damasks and velvets in opposed S-curves.

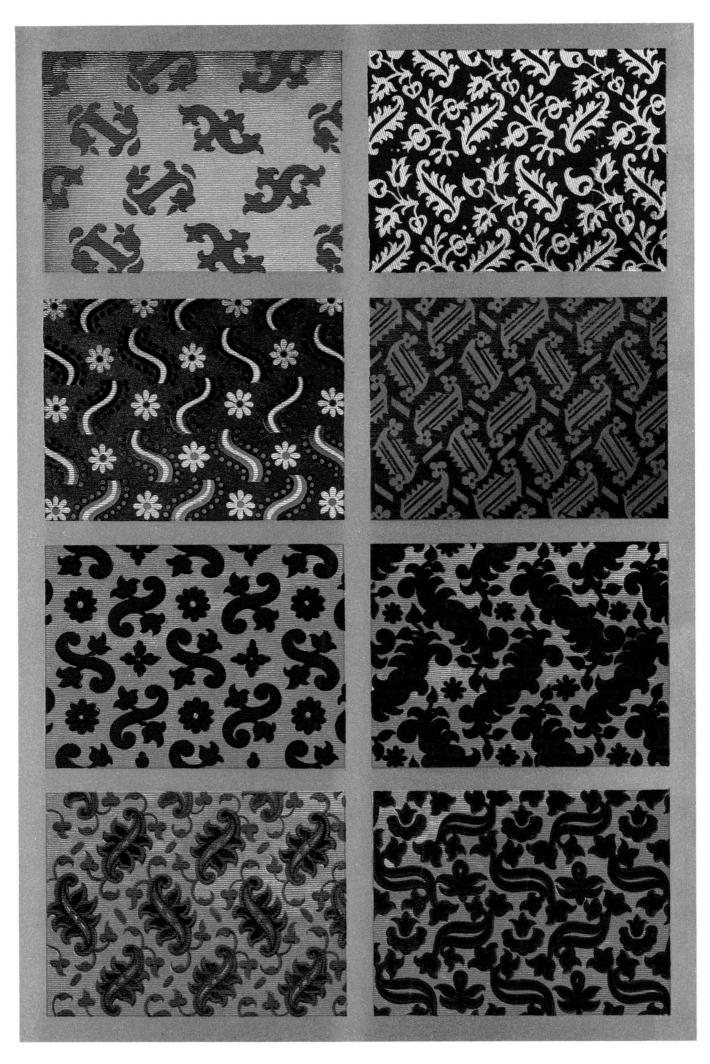

43. Sixteenth century. Zigzagged S-curves.

44. Sixteenth century. Composite patterns with animals affronté.

45. Sixteenth century. Silks with opposed flowers.

46. Sixteenth century. Striped silks, velvets and damasks.

49. Sixteenth and early seventeenth centuries. Silks, damasks and velvets with scrolls decorated with vases and birds.

50. Sixteenth and seventeenth centuries. Fleurs-de-lis.

51. Seventeenth century. Coiled scrolls.

52. Seventeenth century. Running branches in panels.

53. Seventeenth century. Filigreed silks.

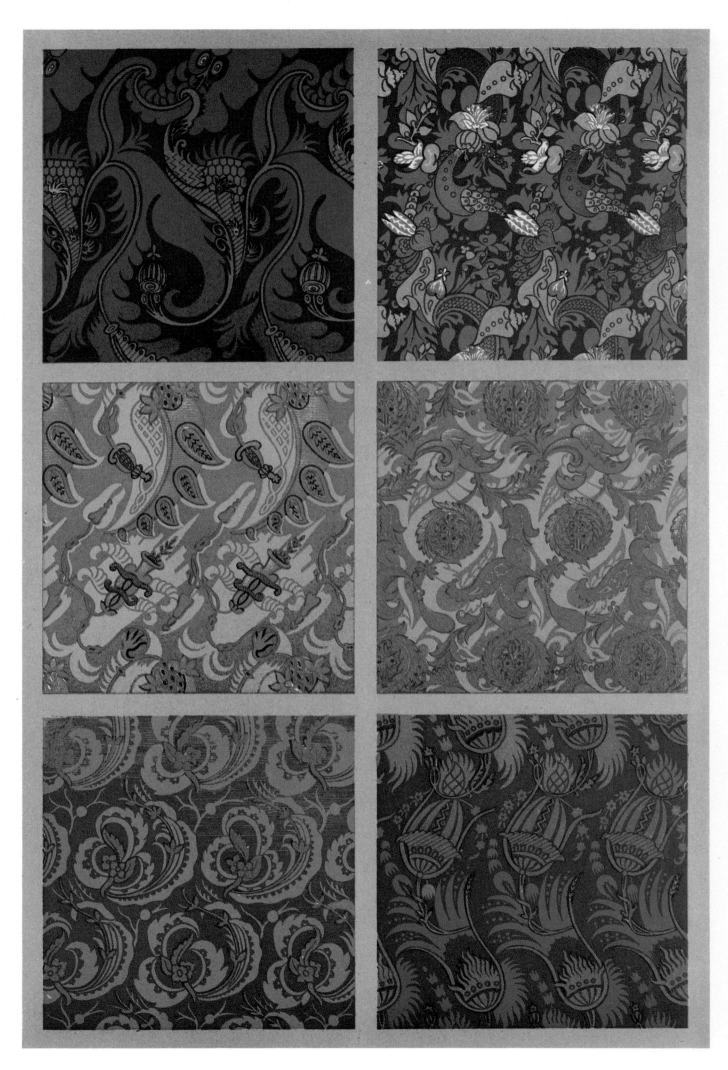

54. Seventeenth century. Imitation Chinese silks made in Venice and Lyons.

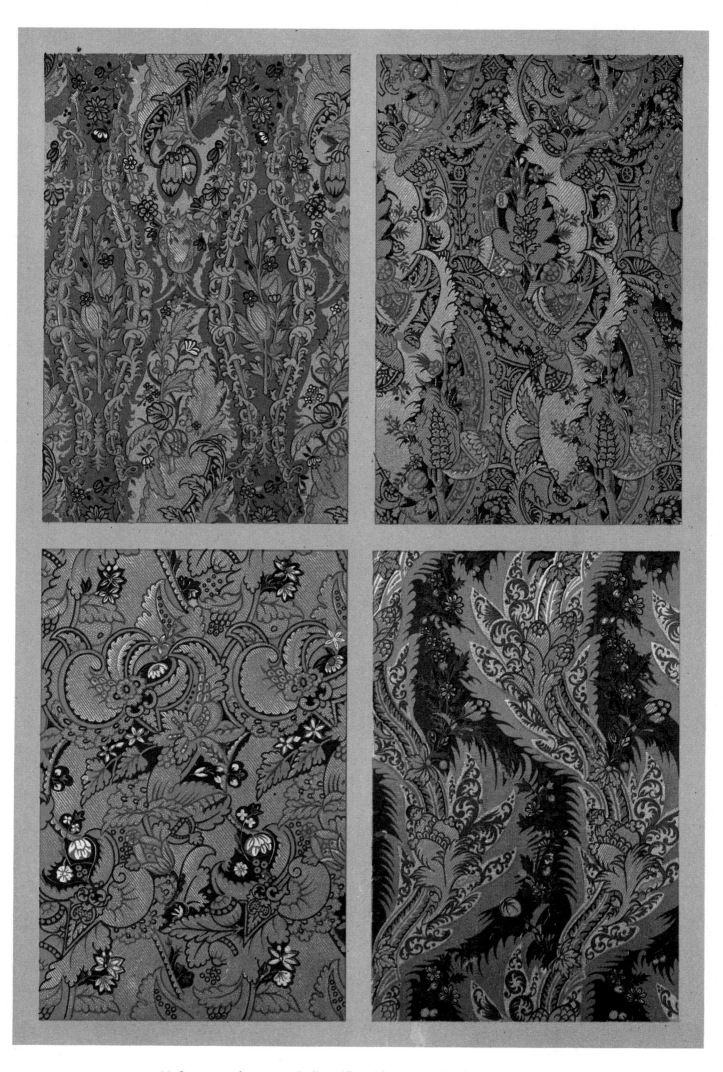

55. Seventeenth century. Italian silks with contorted and serpentine lines.

56. Seventeenth century. Powderings of pomegranates and flowers.

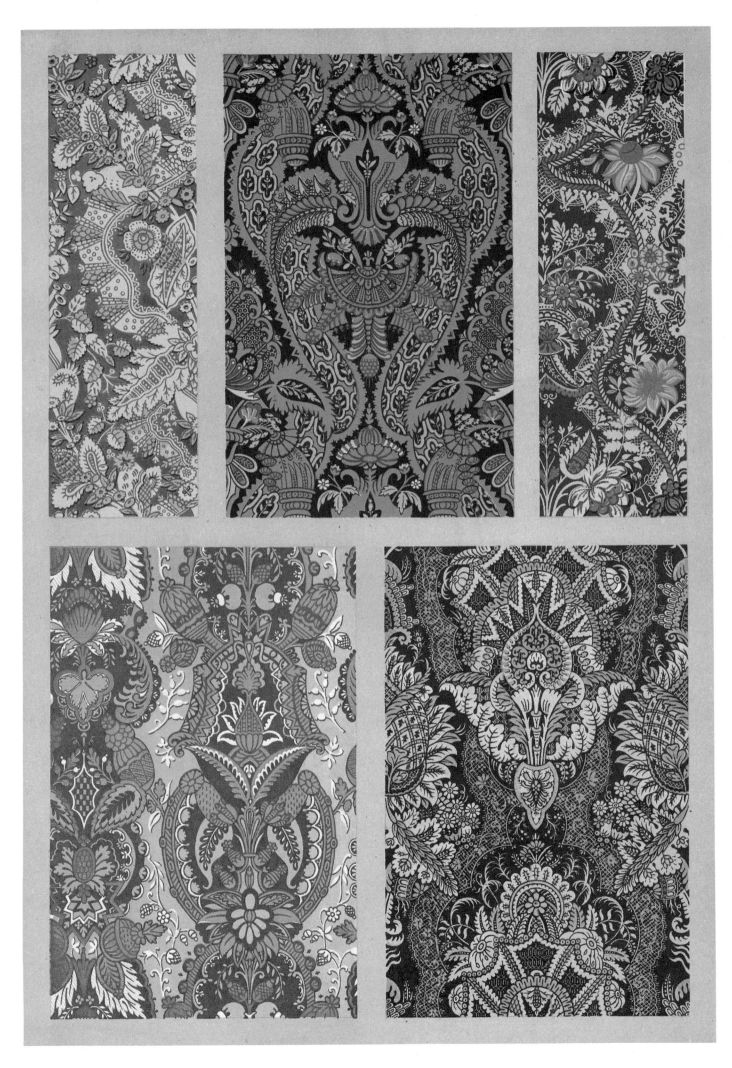

57. Seventeenth century. French dentelated silks.

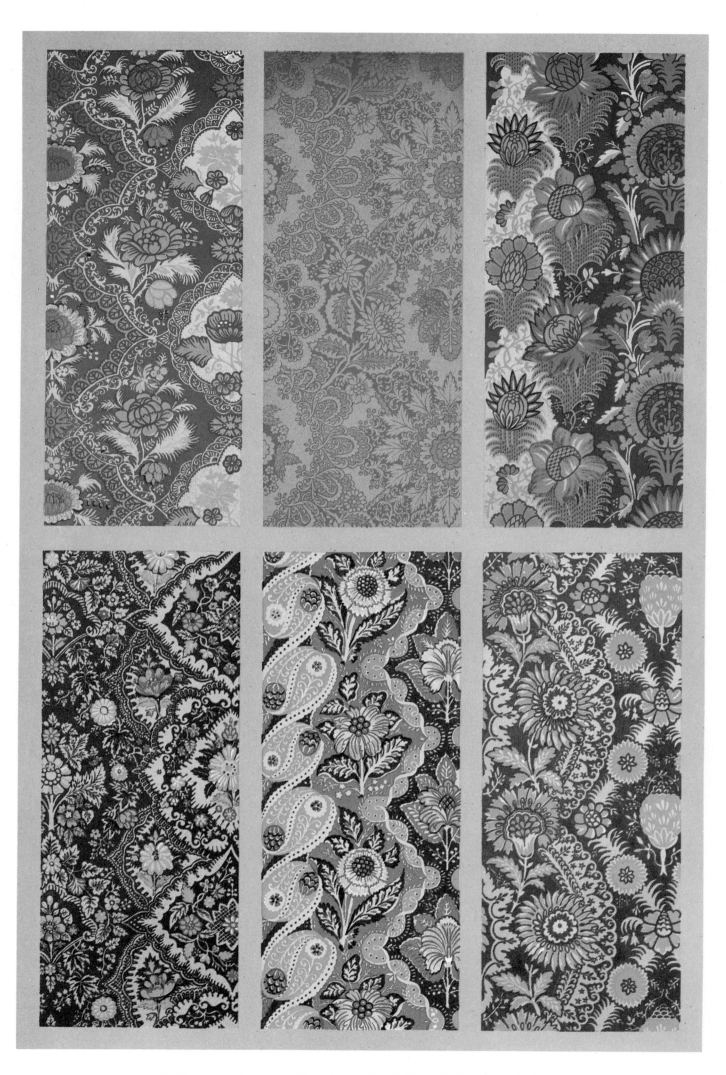

58. Seventeenth century. French dentelated silks with floral powderings.

59. Seventeenth century. Dentelated silks.

60. Seventeenth century. French dentelated silks with pomegranates.

63. Seventeenth century. Silks with vases.

64. Seventeenth century. Many-flowered silks, called "the garden."

65. Seventeenth century. Birds in flight and resting.

66. End of the seventeenth century. Rocaille.

67. Seventeenth century. Brocaded damask in running ribbons.

68. Eighteenth century. Imitation of Chinese silks.

69. Eighteenth century. Coquillage.

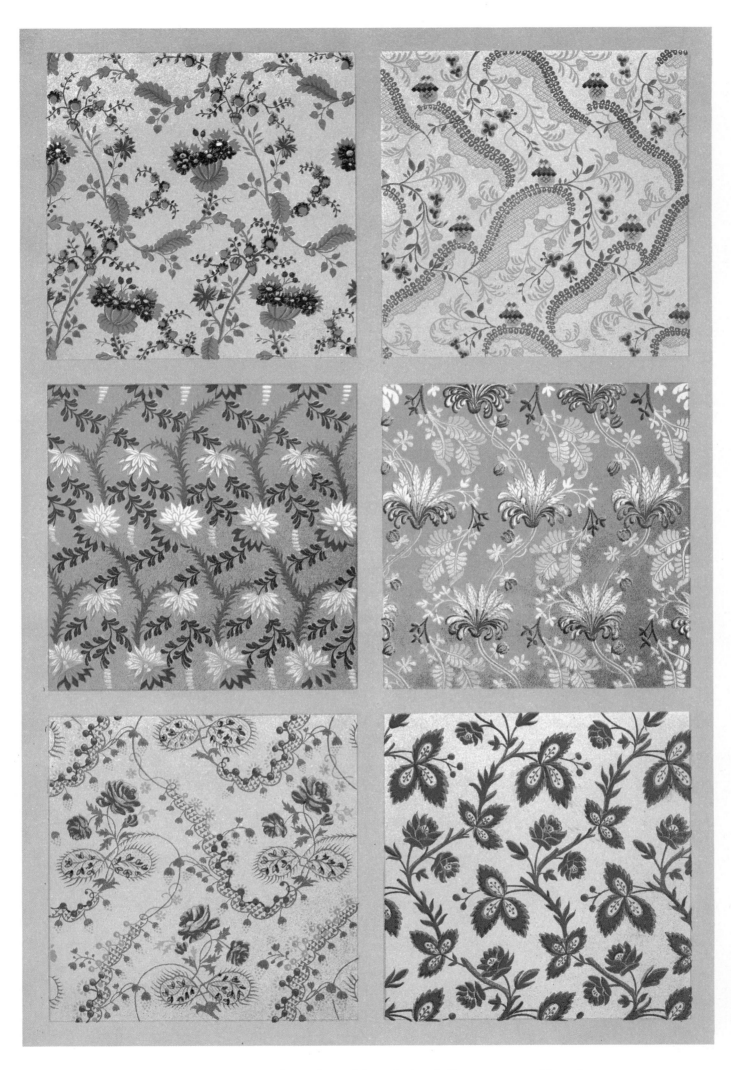

70. Eighteenth century. Silks, satins and damasks in winding patterns and branches.

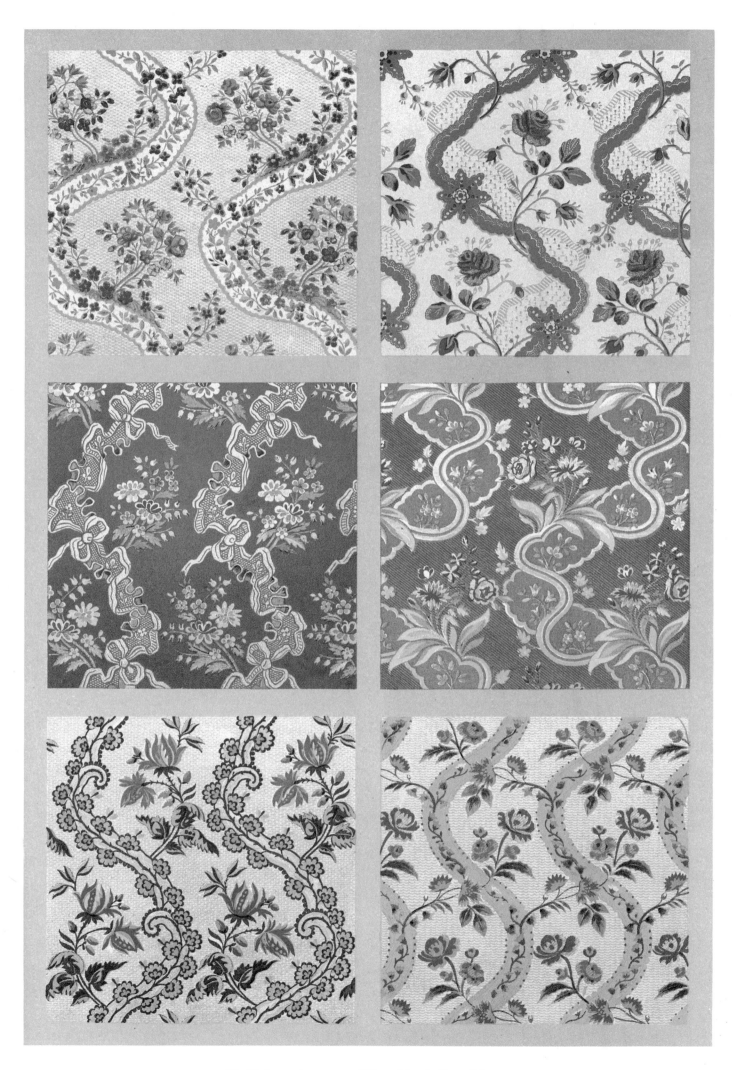

71. Eighteenth century. Silks with winding ribbons.

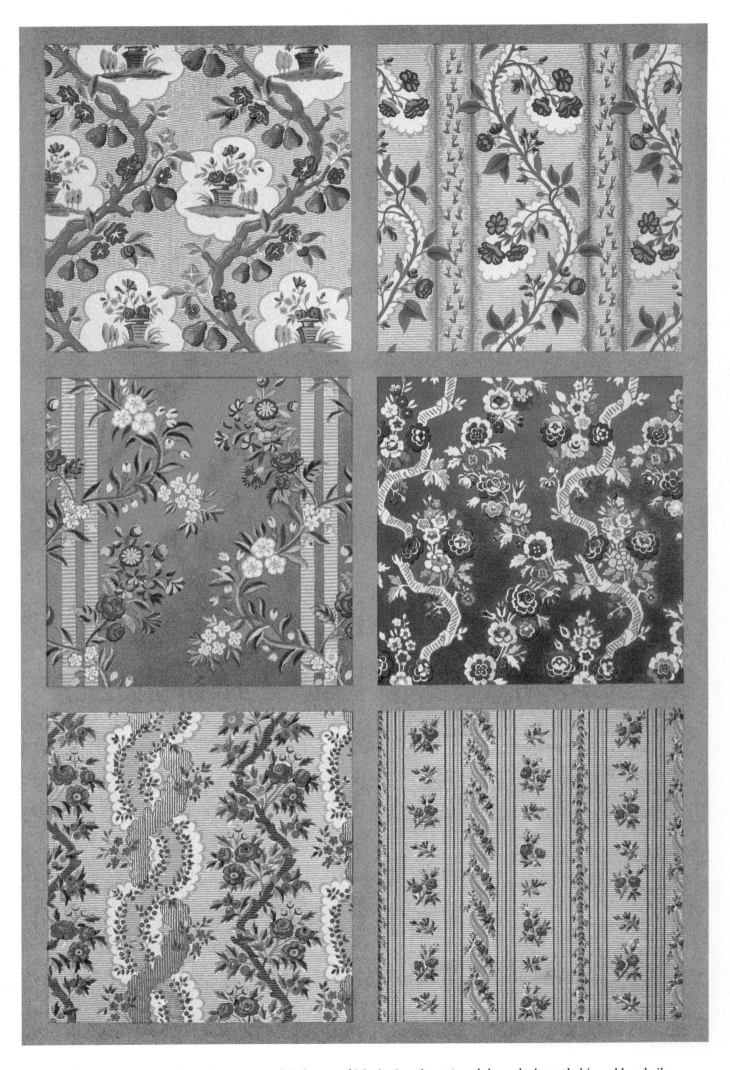

72. Eighteenth century. Dauphines (named in honor of Marie-Antoinette) and damasks brocaded in gold and silver.

73. Eighteenth century. French silks in feathered patterns.

74. Eighteenth century. Pastoral symbols.

75. Eighteenth century. Divisions with flowers.

76. Eighteenth century. Silks with interlaced ribbons.

77. End of the eighteenth century. Circular medallions.

78. Eighteenth century. Silks with panels of ornamental volutes.

79. Eighteenth century. French silks in straight stripes.

80. End of the eighteenth and nineteenth centuries. Pompeian designs (French Consulate and Empire).

81. Fourteenth to the beginning of the seventeenth centuries. Fabrics of wool and wool blends.

82. Sixteenth to eighteenth centuries. Fabrics of wool and wool blends.

83. Eighth to thirteenth centuries. Carolingian and medieval embroideries.

84. Fourteenth and fifteenth centuries. Gothic embroideries.

85. Sixteenth century. Italian Renaissance appliqué.

86. Sixteenth century. Embroidered Renaissance bed valance.

87. Sixteenth century. Appliqué.

88. Sixteenth century. Bed of Henri II.

89. Sixteenth century. Spanish appliqué.

90. Sixteenth century. Italian appliqué.

91. Sixteenth century. Spanish embroidery.

92. Sixteenth century. Spanish appliquéd scrolls.

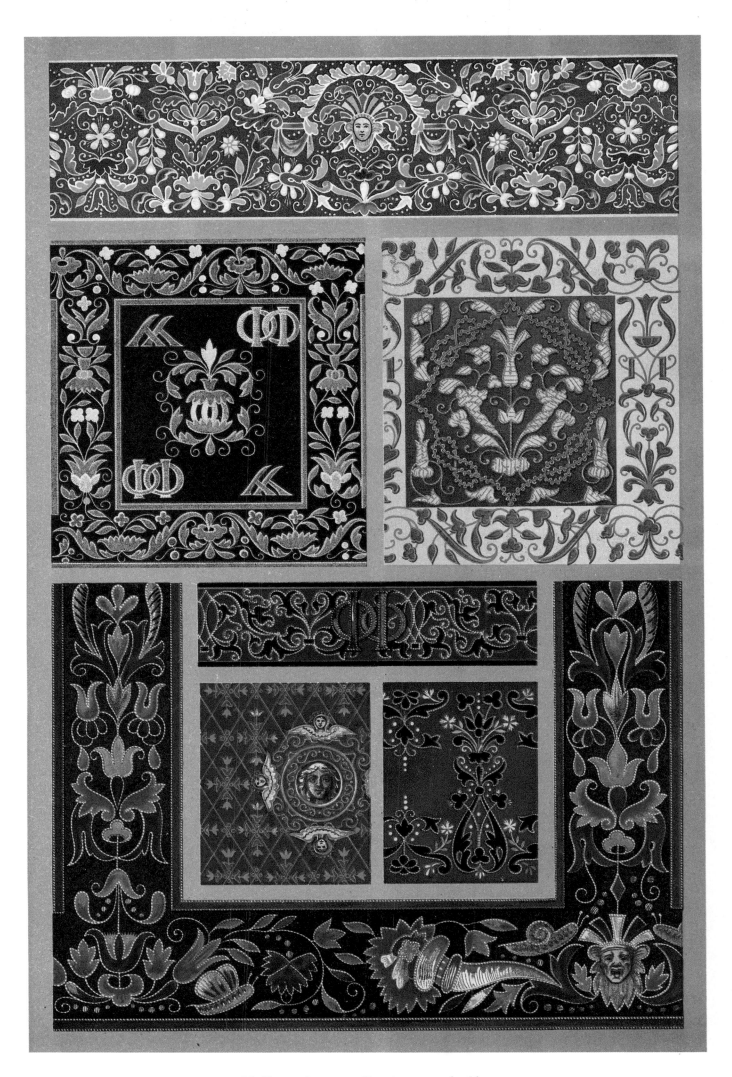

93. Sixteenth century. Renaissance embroidery.

94. Seventeenth century. Flat embroidery without reverse.

95. Eighteenth century. German embroidery.

96. Fifteenth century. Various Persian trimmings.

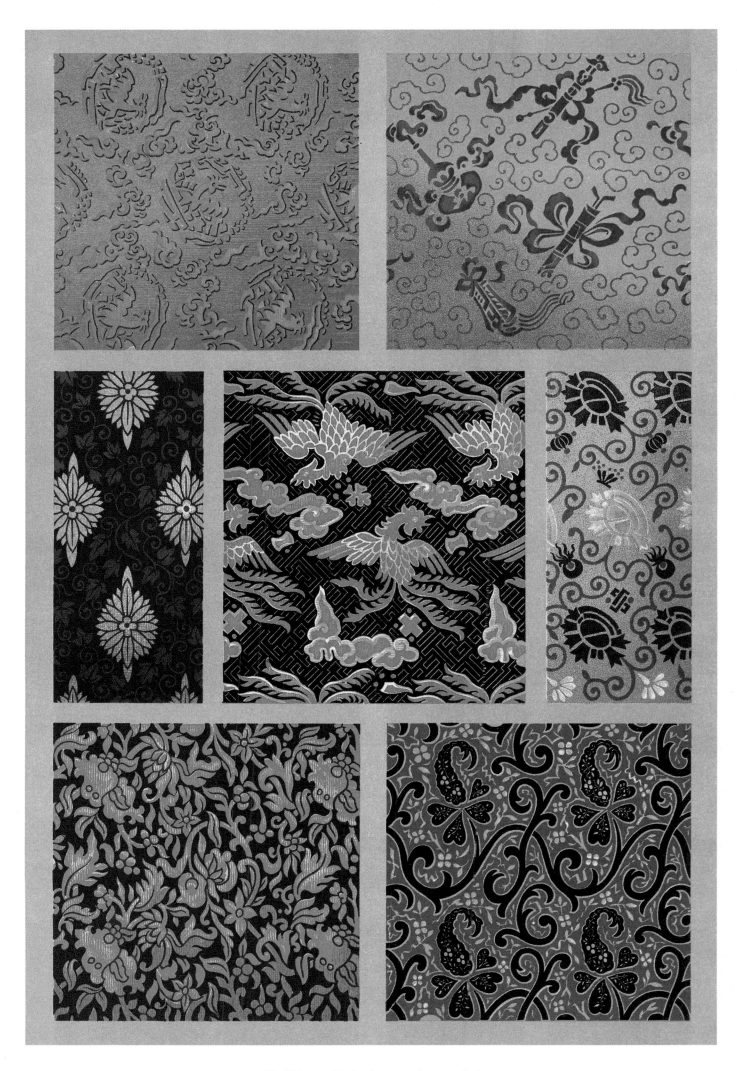

97. Chinese fabrics from various periods.

98. Fifteenth century. Persian fabrics.